Listening to **Leaders**

Why Should I Listen to MY LIBRARIAN?

Christine Honders

PowerKiDS press™

NEW YORK

Published in 2020 by The Rosen Publishing Group, Inc.
29 East 21st Street, New York, NY 10010

Editor: Greg Roza
Book Design: Rachel Rising

Photo Credits: Cover (insert) Bullstar/Shutterstock.com; Cover (background) DavidPinoPhotography/Shutterstock.com; pp. 5, 11, 15 Tyler Olson/Shutterstock.com; p. 7 Rawpixel.com/Shutterstock.com; p. 9 Africa Studio/Shutterstock.com; pp. 13, 21 wavebreakmedia/Shutterstock.com; p. 17 Stephen Simpson Inc/Blend Images/Getty Images; p. 19 © iStockphoto.com/RiverNorthPhotography; p. 22 gualtiero boffi/Shutterstock.com.

Cataloging-in-Publication Data

Names: Honders, Christine.
Title: Why should I listen to my librarian? / Christine Honders.
Description: New York : PowerKids Press, 2020. | Series: Listening to leaders
Identifiers: ISBN 9781538341643 (pbk.) | ISBN 9781538341667 (library bound) | ISBN 9781538341650 (6 pack)
Subjects: LCSH: Librarians--Juvenile literature. | Libraries--Juvenile literature.
Classification: LCC Z682.H66 2019 | DDC 020.92--dc23

Manufactured in the United States of America

CPSIA Compliance Information: Batch #CSPK19 For further information contact Rosen Publishing, New York, New York at 1-800-237-9932.

Contents

The Leader of the Library

It's time to go to the school library. You look at all the books on the shelves. There are so many! How will you find a book that you like? Ask the librarian. Librarians are in charge of the library and can help you find what you are looking for.

Not Just for Books Anymore

Most people think of books when they think of the library. Libraries also have DVDs of movies and your favorite TV shows. They have computers with free **access** to the Internet. The librarian is an expert at finding information and getting it to the people who need it.

Finders of Information

Librarians help people **research** to find information they're looking for. They know which books to **recommend** and where to find them. They show people how to search the Internet and to make sure that the information they find is true. Librarians also buy new books to make sure the library has the newest information.

The School Librarian

School librarians are busy people. They teach students where to find their favorite books and how to check them out. They show older kids how to research information to write papers and book reports. They hold reading groups for kids just learning how to read.

11

School librarians want to make sure every kid does their best in school. They give extra help to students with their homework. They set up after-school programs like book clubs to **encourage** kids to read for fun. Librarians even work with teachers to help create reading lessons in the classroom.

The Public Library

The public library is a library for the **community**. The librarians keep track of everything in the building. They can also tell you the best place to find the information you need. Librarians are information experts and know about books and websites that you've probably never used before.

A Neighborhood Center

Librarians plan after-school programs, book clubs, games, and craft activities to bring people in the neighborhood together. The librarian also invites people from the community to give free classes to kids and adults. You could take a yoga class, a gardening class, or even learn to speak French right at the public library!

Helping People in Need

Public libraries are free to anyone, and they offer many services. Some offer job search training. This helps people who need to find work. Some library workers help people file their taxes. Many libraries have "bookmobiles." These are trucks that bring books to schools, the **elderly**, and people too sick to leave their homes.

Library Skills

Librarians need to know more than how to check out a book. They must know how to use a computer to do research. They spend lots of time **organizing** information so they can help other people find what they need. Some librarians are experts in history books and work in museums.

Listening Is Learning!

The library is a great place to learn and the librarian is the teacher. There are hundreds of books from which to choose. There are activities for kids and adults of all ages. If there's something you need to know, listen to the librarian. He or she will help you find what you're looking for.

Glossary

access: The ability or permission to enter or use something.

community: The people living in an area and the area itself.

elderly: Past middle age.

encourage: To inspire someone to do well.

organizing: Putting into order.

recommend: To support something as worthy.

research: Getting information on a subject.

Index

Websites

Due to the changing nature of Internet links, PowerKids Press has developed an online list of websites related to the subject of this book. This site is updated regularly. Please use this link to access the list: www.powerkidslinks.com/ltl/librarian